Original title:
The Tangle of Threads

Copyright © 2025 Creative Arts Management OÜ
All rights reserved.

Author: Cameron Blair
ISBN HARDBACK: 978-1-80586-053-2
ISBN PAPERBACK: 978-1-80586-525-4

Stringing Together Souls

In a room where yarn does play,
Knots and loops just sway away,
Colors dance in wild delight,
Woolly gnomes take flight at night.

A kitten pounces, oh what fun,
Chasing strings, she thinks she's won!
But in her chase, she trips and rolls,
Creating chaos, fluffing souls.

Grandma's knitting, counting tight,
Misses stitches, oh what a sight,
She winks and says, with playful cheer,
"I meant to make a hat, my dear!"

In coffee shops, a tangled joke,
Yarnballs rolling, here they poke,
We laugh and weave with hearts aglow,
Such silly threads, where friendships grow.

Ties of the Unknown

Once I tried to tie my shoes,
I made a knot that gave me blues.
A twist, a turn, I pulled too tight,
Now they dance in pure delight.

My cat thought it was a game,
Chasing laces, what a shame!
Around my legs, a circus show,
Who knew my shoes could steal the show!

The Pursuit of Pattern

Socks with stripes and polka dots,
Each day I wear the craziest knots.
Matching colors? What a laugh!
I've got a wardrobe full of gaffs!

I tried to find a theme to wear,
But my closet's a wild affair.
Fashion's flair is never clear,
Each outfit's either bold or sheer!

Weaving Whims

I made a scarf that's two feet wide,
It's bright and wild, a crazy ride!
My grandma said it's quite a sight,
A rainbow threw a snowball fight!

With yarn that twirled and loops that spun,
I crafted art for everyone.
But as I wore it around town,
The neighbors asked, "What's that? A gown?"

Threads of Contradiction

I wore my shirt that's bright and bold,
A tale of colors, stories told.
Yet paired with pants that clash and brawl,
I'm the jester of the shopping mall!

When coats don't match, it's quite the game,
I walk like art, it's all the same.
My wardrobe's chaos, woven doubt,
But laughter's what it's all about!

Twists and Turns of Life

Life's a dance, with steps so weird,
Twists and turns, my feet have fled.
Once I tried to skip with glee,
But tripped on lace, oh woe is me!

A sock was lost, the pants too tight,
In merry chaos, what a sight.
I twirl and spin like a silly sprite,
While tangled threads, they laugh at night.

From Threads to Tapestries

A thread of gold, a thread of blue,
Mixed emotions in every hue.
Stitching laughter, pulling frights,
My quilt's a puzzle, oh what delights!

I weave my tales with yarn and glee,
A patchwork monster, look and see!
It's got three eyes and a crooked grin,
A masterpiece, let the fun begin!

Patterns in the Chaos

In a jumbled heap of colors bright,
I search for order in this fight.
Yet as I tug and pull with pride,
A polka-dotted thing comes alive!

A dash of pink, a splash of green,
Making patterns quite obscene.
With every knot, a giggle's heard,
My chaos sings, it's truly absurd!

Web of Whimsy

In a web of whimsy, I'll reside,
Where ticklish threads seem to collide.
A spider spins a joke or two,
While moths dance by, they giggle too!

Caught in loops of playful dread,
Each strand tells stories, quirkily said.
With shingles of laughter, I shall weave,
In my tangled world, I shall believe!

Splintered Fates

In a world of twisted strings,
Shoelaces trip at every turn.
The cat's chasing my favorite things,
While I'm tangled, feeling quite stern.

Each sock's a rebel on its own,
Hiding from what matches best.
My wardrobe's in a cyclone,
Fashion advice, I must suggest!

Threads of Longing

I knit my dreams with hope and yarn,
A sweater made for two or three.
Instead, I cackle at my blarn,
An octopus in a tree!

With needles flying, stitches bend,
But every row's a riotous chase.
In every twist, there lies a friend,
Though I can't find my coffee place.

A Canvas of Crisscrossed Lives

A canvas stretched, a dance of fate,
Colors splatter like a tease.
Paintbrush in hand, I hesitate,
My masterpiece's a puzzle, please!

With laughter spilling on the floor,
A masterpiece gone off the rails.
Art critics giggle, oh, what a score!
As I untangle all my fails.

Interwoven Wishes

Wishes knotted like my hair,
A magic potion brewed with socks.
Unraveling loops in my despair,
While pirate dreams take all my clocks.

With mischief hidden in the seams,
A jester's hat upon my head.
Life's tangled humor fills my dreams,
As I dance 'round with frivolous dread.

Sagas Stitched in Silence

In a corner, Granny knits,
With needles clacking, oh, what hits!
A sock that's somehow turned to hat,
And no one knows where it is at.

Cats are chasing yarn all day,
While dogs just watch, they think it's play.
An errant stitch, a tangled mess,
Creates a scarf for… our pet, I guess!

Each pattern's marked with her sly grace,
A secret code, a crafty trace.
She laughs and calls it modern art,
With mismatched legs, it's quite the heart!

So here's to all the silly seams,
That turn our hopes into wild dreams.
In silent stitches, laughter found,
With quirks in threads, we're all spellbound.

Interlaced Journeys

Two grandmas in a crafty race,
Both eyeing yarn of vibrant lace.
One knits a blanket, warm and bold,
The other weaves a tale retold.

With every purl, they spin a yarn,
About a goat with quite a charm.
It stole a sock and danced about,
Leaving the neighbors all in doubt!

Through loops and skips, their stories blend,
In needlework, the laughs transcend.
They clash in styles, their laughter rolls,
As patterns go awry, they're both on a stroll.

A tapestry of chuckles grows,
With every thread, their friendship glows.
So here's to journeys woven tight,
With mischief, love, and pure delight!

Unraveling the Past

Oh, let me tell you of a time,
When socks were born without a rhyme.
One simply lost its way to roam,
And now, it prances off alone!

Once knitted with such pure intent,
It surely must have had its bent.
Now here it lies, a sole-some plight,
The partner's gone, it's quite a sight!

The yarn recalls those silly days,
Of tangled threads and wobbly ways.
Each pull a tug, each knot a tale,
As mismatched socks set forth to sail.

So laugh with me at what we've spun,
A history of joy and fun.
In every twist, in every cast,
Beneath the stitches, we unravel past!

Knitting Hearts Together

In a café, they gather round,
With sticks and yarn, their smiles abound.
A project planned to bring them cheer,
Yet patterns mixed, they end up near!

One starts a scarf, another a shade,
But somehow ends in a knot parade.
A mitten turns to sweater odd,
As laughter spills, and winks are prod.

With needles clicking, hearts collide,
As friendship blooms in every stride.
They knit and purl their lives so sweet,
Creating warmth from every beat.

So here's a toast to threads we weave,
In laughter's glow, we do believe.
With every stitch, we find our place,
In tales of yarn, we interlace!

Chasing the Unraveled

Once I had a ball of yarn,
It tumbled down with such a charm.
A chase began, my cat did pounce,
Laughing as she made it bounce.

Around the chairs and under the bed,
That yarn disaster, where angels fear to tread.
I chased it far, I chased it wide,
With every twist, my sanity tried.

In knots and loops, my patience wore,
Yet every tug just caused one more.
Who knew such fun could come from one,
A spool of chaos under the sun?

So here's to yarn and kitty chases,
To funny days and tangled places.
Life's a mess, but what the heck,
I'll laugh it off and just reflect!

Threads of Fate

A needle winked with sly delight,
As threads wove tales from day to night.
Each stitch a giggle, each knot a prank,
I sewed my dreams, then fell in rank.

A fashion show of mismatched flair,
My trousers danced, my shirt a scare.
Who knew that plaid could be so bold?
Or polka dots, so brave and old?

With every twist, a laugh arose,
Stitching life with ups and throes.
A tailor's whim, a seamstress' jest,
In fashion folly, I feel so blessed.

Through tangles tight, I find my stride,
In threads of fate, I take my ride.
So when life frays, with colors wide,
I wear my laughter as my pride!

Entangled Dreams

I dreamt of yarn that danced at night,
In colors bright, what a goofy sight.
They twirled and spun like ballerinas,
Tangled thoughts in wooly arenas.

A sweater made of wishes rare,
I wore it once, but it wasn't fair.
For every wish to keep me warm,
It snagged my heart in yarny charm.

In dreams I weave a world so wild,
Where patterns laugh, and needles smiled.
Each twist and turn a funny quirk,
In tangled dreams, I find my perk.

So let's embrace this woven fate,
With threads of laughter, let's not be late.
For life is but a silly seam,
So join me now, let's chase the dream!

Knots of Memory

With every knot, a tale to tell,
Of socks gone missing, oh so well.
I find them tucked in odd places,
A game of hide and seek embraces.

My memories tied in yarn so bright,
A sweater whispering through the night.
"Remember that time?" it seems to say,
As stitches giggle, come what may.

A tangled mess, yet so profound,
In knots of memory, joy is found.
I laugh and sigh at every thread,
Each woven time, a dance instead.

As I unloop the yarny past,
I find the funny moments last.
So here's to knots, both tight and free,
In tangled tales, there's joy for me!

Wefts of Wonder

In a world of colors bright,
Strings of laughter take their flight.
Jumbled knots in playful spree,
Ticklish twists, oh, can't you see?

Ribbons dance in silly loops,
Naughty threads and goofy troops.
Wobbly patterns make us grin,
A garish mess that's sure to win.

Fuzzy fuzz and yarn so bold,
Spinning tales both new and old.
With each twist, a chuckle grows,
Every stitch, a comic prose.

Jesters thread in bright parade,
Silly antics, never fade.
In this weave of giggles spun,
Life's a laugh, let's have some fun!

Patterns of Solitude

Lonely fibers twist and turn,
Yearning for a friend to learn.
Single strands in quiet night,
Whisper tales of odd delight.

They tangle up without a care,
Wishing someone else was there.
But in silence, goofy pranks,
Unravel laughable outcranks.

Serene knots with secret jokes,
Talking threads with funny pokes.
In solitude, they still amuse,
Witty weaves that one can use.

Soon the thread finds company,
A dance of yarn in harmony.
From lonely to a jolly feast,
In patterns shared, joy's unleashed!

Woven Whispers

Whispers of yarn flit in the air,
Tickling toes with silly flair.
Stories stitched in laughter rhyme,
Woven tunes, a jester's chime.

Fleeting whispers, light and grand,
Threads of giggles twist and strand.
Wobbly whispers, oh what fun,
In a tapestry we've begun.

Jolly fibers softly tease,
Dancing under playful breeze.
In stitches made by jovial hands,
Laughter echoes through the lands.

Woven giggles, never shy,
Each thread a trick, oh my, oh my!
In the cloth of silly dreams,
Every strand bursts at the seams!

Frayed Ends and New Beginnings

Frayed ends dangle, what a sight,
Hoping for a friendly bite.
Tangles pull at every seam,
In this comedy, we dream.

A twist, a turn, a knot so grand,
Unruly yarn just takes a stand.
Every snag brings forth a laugh,
In our joyful, jumbled craft.

New beginnings from the shreds,
Funny tales that dance in heads.
Fiber fluffs with cheeky pride,
In this chaos, fun will ride.

So gather up the threads today,
Let's weave together, come what may.
With frayed ends, we make our way,
To find the humor in the play!

The Stitch that Holds

In a world where yarns collide,
Socks are lost, oh where they hide!
A button pops, it dares to flee,
My sewing skills? A mystery!

Needles dancing, sharp and spry,
I thread them well, or at least I try.
A patchwork heart, stitched with glee,
Still, I trip on yarn, oh me!

Embracing the Knot

A twist and turn, a playful fight,
My shoelaces wrangle with delight.
Caught in loops that never end,
My foot's new friend, a long-lost mend!

Hubby says, "Just tie them tight!"
I laugh; his knots are quite the sight.
In chaos, love finds its way,
As I trip over laces every day!

Silhouettes in Silk

Silk slips by, a sneaky sprite,
Creeping into my clothes at night.
Oh, who knew fabric had such flair?
It dances 'round without a care!

With every thread, a tale unfolds,
Of fashion fails and treasures bold.
A snug silk scarf, oh what a show,
I wore it wrong—no one would know!

Fragile Fibers

A threadbare shirt, my favorite yet,
With holes that let the cool winds fret.
I patched it up with tape and glue,
Fashion faux pas? I just can't do!

When fibers scream, I laugh and sigh,
A dance of drapery catching my eye.
The fragile threads weave tales anew,
Of laundry drops and moments true!

Weaving Time's Stories

In a loom of laughter, tales are spun,
Like socks mismatched, but oh what fun!
Knots of memory form a quirky dance,
Each thread a giggle, a silly chance.

Warped and weft, our moments collide,
With every tug, we take a ride.
Woven with whimsy, yarns intertwine,
A tapestry of joy, oh, how divine!

The Fabric of Connection

Among the fibers, friendships play,
In stitches of humor, we find our way.
Twist and turn, a playful thread,
Sewing the laughter in all that's said.

Quirky patterns on life's old scheme,
In patches of smiles, we stitch our dream.
Every loop a chuckle, every knot a cheer,
Binding us closer, bringing us near.

Strands of Serendipity

Serendipitous moments, a tangled spree,
A mishap with yarn leads to glee!
Unraveled and jumbled, a colorful mess,
But in laughter we find, it's all a success.

Each twist and turn, a story unfolds,
In the fabric of life, there are gold threads told.
Mismatched socks, and hats that don't fit,
But in this chaos, we revel a bit.

Echoes in the Weave

In the clatter of needles, echoes ring,
A chorus of joy that we all can sing.
Threads that shimmer with stories of yore,
Tantalizing tales, always asking for more.

Weaving the quirks of our days with zest,
In the fabric of laughter, we find our best.
A patchwork of moments, stitched with delight,
In this crazy quilt, everything feels right!

Weaving Through Time

In a loom of laughter, we spin and sway,
Chasing silly shadows, come what may.
Yarns of silly stories, bright and wild,
Each stitch a giggle, like a playful child.

Threading through ages, clip and clop,
Every weave makes time do a hop.
Nostalgia in colors, stripes that tease,
A patchwork quilt that brings you to your knees.

From retro sweaters to socks gone wrong,
Every frayed hem holds a tale so strong.
We dance in fibers, twirling around,
In this yarn of moments, joy is found.

So let's tangle and twist, giggles galore,
In the fabric of life, always explore.
With needles and laughter, we craft our plight,
Weaving through time, it's a comical sight!

The Disguise of Threads

Once a sober thread, in tone so gray,
Decided to dress up, in a fanciful way.
With polka dots and sparkles, a grand debut,
It danced around, confusing the blue.

Stitch after stitch, it tangled and twirled,
Soon every fabric was gleefully swirled.
A bow here, a button there, what a wild spree,
Each outfit a riot, oh what a sight to see!

Thread that pretends it's something elite,
Found its new place on a cat's little feet.
Draped in a costume, oh what a tease,
Silly little thread, do whatever you please!

When the seams start to giggle, we'll know it's true,
Threads in disguise make the best of a brew.
A parade of fabrics, can't help but cheer,
In the carnival of stitches, fun does appear!

Knots of Courage

In a world of tangles, we tie our fate,
Knots of courage, never to berate.
With every slip, and every pull tight,
We learn to laugh beneath our fright.

Bows and twists, a clumsy ballet,
Yet each knot whispers, "You'll be okay."
Embracing the chaos, we dance on the line,
Happiness weaves through each silly design.

Overhand, square, and a butterfly flair,
Our threads of resolve fill the air.
Tangled together, we face our fears,
Knots full of giggles, soaked in our tears.

So grab that thread, let's tie it anew,
With laughter as glue, we'll make it through.
No unraveling here, we're brave little ants,
In knots of courage, we'll do our happy dance!

Chords of Connection

Strummed a little thread, oh what a sound,
Weaving a melody, joy all around.
With laughter as rhythm, we twist and we spin,
Creating a chorus where friendships begin.

Each string a life lesson, a jester's tune,
Tangled in laughter, beneath the moon.
Chords of connection, in chaos they meet,
A symphony crafted, oh how sweet!

With each playful tug, the music will soar,
These threads of our tales open every door.
Fumbled notes and giggles, it's all part of play,
In life's funny concert, let's dance away!

From banter to banjo, we're strumming it right,
A tapestry woven with joy and delight.
So raise your glasses, let the story unfold,
In chords of connection, the laughter is gold!

Fragments of an Interwoven Tale

In a cupboard, socks start to fight,
One claims it's always in the right.
In the corner, buttons gossip away,
How dull it gets on a rainy day.

A shoelace dances with a stray thread,
Mocks the napkin that lies in bed.
Chasing crumbs like a starving cat,
While the lint roller plots with a hat.

A spool of yarn yawns with a sigh,
Wonders if it's time to fly high.
While the paper clips twist with delight,
Dreaming of tales under the moonlight.

Oh, what chaos in a drawer's seam,
As mismatched bits weave a silly dream.

The Color of Connections

Red thread laughs, it's always bold,
Saying, 'Come on, let's be gold!'
While blue string rolls its eyes in dismay,
'Who chose this color for today?'

Green ribbons sway with a giggle or two,
'Can you believe the things we do?'
And purple beads, they shake with cheer,
Planning a party that's drawing near.

Yellow threads whisper of sunlit skies,
While black twine dreams of mysterious ties.
Each hue a character, funny and bright,
Painting a picture of chaos and light.

In this vibrant web, friendship's the dance,
Where laughter blooms, giving chaos a chance.

Entwined Histories

Once a needle was caught in a yarn,
Making its way through each tiny barn.
It told a tale of a missing sock,
As the thimble laughed at the clock.

Elastic bands stretched with a grin,
'Fitting in? Oh, where to begin?
While safety pins tried to take the lead,
Claiming their duty was quite the deed.

Old gloves chimed in with stories of warmth,
Saying, 'We've seen better days, forsooth!'
Amid the clatter of buttons and threads,
They punctuated laughs with their heads.

In this grand tangle, the oddest of friends,
Each stitch a giggle, where laughter transcends.

Stitches of Solitude

In a quiet room, a thread took a nap,
Dreaming of patterns and a wide map.
A needle peeked in, poked and prodded,
'Hope you dream of something a bit lauded!'

A lonely seam sighed from the floor,
'These stitches of solitude are a bore.'
But suddenly, a scissor cut in fast,
'Let's make this party a blast!'

Friends came flocking, all colors aligned,
Twisting and tumbling, a mess designed.
The bobbin rolled in with a quirky cheer,
Shouting, 'Let's stitch up some fun right here!'

At day's end, the laughter was spun,
In the fabric of friendships, all came undone.

Shadows in the Loom

In a world where colors clash,
A sock is missing, oh what a smash!
The objects dance, they twist and shout,
Who knew a laundry could cause such doubt?

With tangled yarns and giggles galore,
The cat leaps high, a crafty explorer.
Spools roll round like a circus act,
While socks conspire, how bizarre! In fact!

With sticky fingers, I pull at the threads,
A blanket of chaos, where logic dreads.
The knitter chuckles, embers glow bright,
In this wobbly world, laughter takes flight.

So here we dance, with knits in a whirl,
In a fabric of folly, we twirl and twirl.
As laughter unravels each stitch and seam,
In the loom's funny shadows, we live our dream.

Knotted Realities

A ball of twine rolls down the lane,
It trips, it falls—oh, what a pain!
My project's growing like a wild vine,
Each twist and turn, I'm losing my mind!

With mismatched patches, my quilt's a show,
It looks more like a taco, though!
Threading my thoughts, I tie a knot,
And hope like crazy it holds what I've got.

The fabric rejects my pixel clan,
Stitching and glitching, a tangled plan.
With every loop, I hope for grace,
But the needle's laughing—what a data race!

So I cuddle my blanket, lumpy and bright,
It's quirky and funny, a pure delight.
In this knotted reality, let's raise a cheer,
For all the wonky wonders we hold so dear!

Threads of Remembrance

Grandma's sweater with patches of cheer,
Each stitch a story, memories dear.
With every fray, and every torn seam,
We laugh at the tales that knitters can deem.

A button gone rogue, an elbow to space,
Where did it run off? In which time and place?
I sipped my tea while unraveling fate,
Knitting nostalgia, it's never too late.

The yarn throws a party, it gets out of hand,
A cacophony of colors, oh, isn't it grand?
With each awkward twist, memories collide,
In the fabric of laughter, we surely abide.

Threads of remembrance, a festival bright,
With knots of joy and cozy delight.
So let's raise our needles, let laughter extend,
To all of the stories that yarns can pretend!

Tangled Emotions

A twist of fate in my sewing basket,
Each thread a feeling, some good and some brash.
With laughter, I stitch up a frown or a grin,
Who knew crafting could bring out that din?

Emotions run wild, a chaotic spree,
Butterflies and brambles, oh what a spree!
The fabric of life is a whimsical dance,
In tangled threads, we might take a chance.

With every stitch, I tie up my woes,
A quilt of giggles, that's how it goes!
So let's gather round, let the needles fly,
In this colorful mess, we laugh and sigh.

Tangled emotions, let's embrace the fuss,
In the art of creation, we put our trust.
So here's to the fun, the joy in the knit,
For in tangled threads, we find our wit!

Fragments of Fabric

A sock escapes, a seam's undone,
A quilted map of lost and fun.
Threads that dart and weave like street,
Who knew a button could have feet?

The lint parade, a cozy show,
In pockets deep, where fluff must grow.
With scissors poised, a daring snip,
To craft a cap, a wobbly trip!

A sweater's tale, a tale of cheer,
Its yarns are tangled, never fear.
In every knot, a laugh we find,
A fabric story, so unrefined!

So here's to fibers, wild and free,
In this mad weave, come laugh with me.
For in each stitch, a twist of fate,
A patchwork life that's truly great!

The Dance of Fibers

Two threads do tango, round and round,
Their clumsy shuffle, quite profound.
One takes a leap, the other slips,
And off they go on tangled trips!

A patchwork quilt, a dizzy dance,
With every squiggle, there's a chance.
To craft a pocket, or a hat,
These fibers jive, imagine that!

A needle pricks, a playful poke,
As one thread whispers, 'Are you broke?'
They spin and twirl, what a delight,
In this fine circus, what a sight!

As fabrics sashay under moonlight,
Their tangled ballet feels so right.
In every twist, a giggle grows,
The waltz of fibers forever flows!

Colorful Confusions

A patch of red meets green with blue,
In crafts that seem to misconstrue.
A polka dot in plaid's embrace,
Laughing at their mismatched grace!

A fabric festival, bright and loud,
With stitches forming raucous crowd.
Patterns clash and colors fight,
Who said fashion needs to be right?

A ribbon flies, a bow gone wild,
In fabric land, we're all beguiled.
With every snip, a chuckle springs,
As chaos reigns in what it brings!

So dive into this vibrant mess,
Embrace the clashing, nothing less.
For in confusion, joy we find,
A craft that's playful, sweet, and kind!

Patterns in Chaos

In a world where stitches undecide,
And patterns roam with reckless pride.
Each fabric swirls, like kids at play,
In this grand game of 'Who's to say?'

A plaid bow ties with a striped sock,
Tickling styles with every knock.
Each measure's mad, a math gone wrong,
Yet laughter blooms in this fabric song!

A button now joins a furry thread,
In mismatched glory, never dread.
They prance about, making a fuss,
In this odd ensemble, what's the plus?

So let them dance, this joyful march,
Though patterns clash, they form their arch.
In every stitch, a story glows,
Chaos reigns where laughter grows!

Winding Paths and Weaving Dreams

In a garden of socks, all mismatched and bright,
The washing machine laughs, oh what a sight!
Each fiber a story, a wild, wavy dance,
With hangers and pegs, they all take their stance.

A knitted cat jumps in a leap that's quite bold,
Chasing down yarn that has turned into gold.
With needles and purls, the laughter ensues,
As stitches unite in a game they all choose.

The buttons get rowdy, each with a quirk,
They shimmy and shake, oh, what a great perk!
With twirls and tickles, they never feel dread,
In the land of the tangled, where humor is fed.

They weave tales together, so silly and bright,
A tapestry spun with delight and with light.
In this whimsical mess, they don't want to rest,
For in every knot lies a joke that's the best!

The Network of Being

In a web of connections, where odd friends reside,
A toaster and blanket throw parties with pride.
They gossip in currents, they twinkle with glee,
As crumbs form a dance floor, come join the spree!

The couch cushions gather, they bicker and pout,
As popcorn kernels pop, they all jump about.
With laughter that bubbles and spills on the floor,
This network of beings, who could ask for more?

A clock chimes a tune, though the hour's a mess,
It's hard to pick favorites in such a finesse.
They wobble and wobble, oh, what a delight,
This chorus of chaos, both silly and bright.

In this world so absurd, all tangled and fun,
Each thread weaves a story, a race never run.
So join in the laughter, the friendships that cling,
In the network of life, oh, what joy they bring!

Patterns of the Heart

A button-eyed bear watches socks in a race,
Each pair with a mission, an odd sense of grace.
With stripes and with polka dots dancing around,
They spin in a circle, a whimsical sound.

The bow ties are arguing, comparing their flair,
While slippers are teasing with a wobbly dare.
In this patchwork of pride, they shuffle and sway,
Creating a pattern where laughter holds sway.

The threads start to tangle, they giggle and shout,
With every twist woven, they're never without.
Each stitch tells a joke, each loop brings a cheer,
In this fabric of fun, it's all crystal clear.

So gather your garments, let's jump in the fray,
With patterns that tickle, they brighten the day.
In the world of the thread, where humor takes part,
We stitch up our lives, with love in the heart!

Ties that Define Us

In a world of loose ends, tangled up tight,
Where shoelaces squabble, and socks start to fight.
A belt makes a stand, it's quite the delight,
Holding everyone close, keeping snug through the night.

The mittens are arguing, who's warmer than who?
While hats on their heads create quite the hullabaloo.
In this jumble of fabrics, a friendship does grow,
With laughter unending, they steal quite the show.

When ties meet with laughter, and laughter with glee,
These fabric-bound friends share their silly esprit.
With a twist and a turn, they all gather near,
In the joy of connection, we hold most dear.

So let's tie ourselves up, in this funny affair,
With stitches of mirth and a love that we share.
In this quirky embrace, we find who we are,
In the twist of the fabric, we all shine like stars!

Sewing the Unknown

In a world where needles dance,
Fabrics twist with strange romance.
Buttons giggle, threads take flight,
Sewing mishaps bring delight.

Bobbin's hiding, throwing shades,
Scissors laughing in charades.
Pin cushions bounce with silly cheer,
Stitching tales we hold so dear.

Mismatched socks begin to scheme,
Fabric fairies fuel the dream.
We stitch and laugh 'til fingers ache,
Who knew a quilt could be so fake?

Threads end up tangled in my hair,
A patchwork creature, quite a scare.
But in this mess, we simply grin,
Sewing the unknown, let the fun begin!

Entwined Souls

Two spools spinning, what a sight,
Caught in chaos, day and night.
Needles prickle, threads collide,
In this mess we take great pride.

Unruly loops, like playful cats,
Stitch by stitch, we share our hats.
A needle's wink, a thread's embrace,
We find our groove in this crazy space.

Bobbins roll and fabrics fall,
We dance around the crafting hall.
Between the stitches, laughter flows,
Entwined lives, as everyone knows.

In mismatched seams, we find our groove,
With every stitch, our worries remove.
Stitchin' stories, hearts anew,
Entwined souls, me and you!

Snags in Serenity

In a peaceful room, so neat and prim,
A thread gets caught, oh where to begin?
The fabric sighs; it tugs and pulls,
Snags in serenity, creating stools.

Buttons play hide and seek with ease,
They giggle behind the sewing peas.
As I chase them round the floor,
I miss the needle, oh, what a chore!

Sewing zen turns to playful mess,
Fabric storms lead to pure distress.
Yet in this chaos, laughs emerge,
For snags can spark the joy, submerge.

Each tangled tale a story spun,
Serenity grows with every pun.
In sewing's dance, we find our way,
Snags in life, let's laugh and play!

Threads of an Untold Story

Each thread a tale, untold we weave,
Fabrics whisper, too shy to leave.
With stitches twirling, tales begin,
In this chaos, the fun's a win.

Stray threads wander, lost in dreams,
Patches giggle in hunky schemes.
Hats that flap, a dress that sings,
Creating joy with all these things.

Stitching up a quirky plot,
Laughter bursts in every knot.
In this sewing, strange things appear,
Embracing joy, dismissing fear.

So join the threads in a merry spree,
For every stitch brings glee to thee.
With every fabric, stories bloom,
Threads of an untold story, let joy loom!

Fabric of Dreams

In a quilt of colors, bright and wild,
Lies a patchwork of wishes, dreams compiled.
A thread went missing, oh what a sight,
Bouncing through fabric, taking flight!

Buttons are giggling, seams in a dance,
A needle's lost rhythm, but still, they prance.
Stitches tell stories, some silly, some grand,
In a world where the fabric's simply unplanned.

Yarns spin tall tales of odd sock pairs,
A rogue little scarf, it tickles and cares.
Loopy and twisted, the patterns collide,
In the fabric of dreams, we all take a ride!

So here's to the stitches that laugh and play,
In the seams of our lives, come join the fray.
With needles a-twinkle and threads all around,
In this wacky adventure, laughter is found!

Threads of Yesterday

Old clothes in the closet, stacked up in piles,
Whispering secrets, sharing their smiles.
A button's a storyteller, belt loops chime in,
With tales of the places these threads have been!

The grandma's old apron, embroidered with care,
Has seen many kitchens, with flour in the air.
It chuckles at mishaps, and warns with a wink,
'That time with the cake? Just don't even think!'

A sock and a mitten, lost in their quest,
Both claiming they're better, but who's the best dressed?
With patches and colors, oh what a sight,
They argue and banter, oh what pure delight!

So gather your treasures, the fabrics so frail,
For laughter can echo in each little tale.
Threads of yesterday, spun with a cheer,
Are the fabric of laughter that brings us near!

Echoes in Yarn

Yarns weave together in whispers and giggles,
Knots that are tangled, they twist and they wriggle.
A ball of bright colors rolls 'round for a look,
As sweaters have secrets, just like a good book!

The camel is knitting while sipping some tea,
Much to the sheep's mischief, 'Oh just let it be!'
Purls and knit stitches get caught in the fray,
As they humor each other, bound to delay!

A broomstick got jealous of grandma's fresh shawl,
It jumped in the mix, and made quite a call.
With laughter and yarn, oh what a weave,
In a world of good humor, you just can't believe!

So listen for echoes in yarn that will sing,
Of the fun that each fiber is destined to bring.
In our playful spool dance, we all find our part,
As yarn-spirations laugh, oh it warms the heart!

Woven Secrets

Behind every thread, there's a giggling tale,
Of mischief and laughter, woven without fail.
The loom creaks a laugh, as it spins and it shakes,
At all the wild patterns and quirks that it makes.

A rogue little fiber sneaks under the weave,
Tickling the surface, as everyone grieves!
The fabric can't stop all the odd little pranks,
With threads that decide they need to make tanks!

Dresses in line-ups compare their fine lace,
While the moth in the corner just wants a warm space.
With so much commotion, who knows what will bloom,
In the world of stitched fabric that dances in the room!

So marvel at fibers, both funky and neat,
For every woven secret just can't take a seat.
With laughter and whimsy, the needles do twirl,
In the threads of creation, we've made quite a whirl!

Loops of Longing

In a sock drawer, a quest for a mate,
Yet I find a sock that's stuck in the crate.
Running in circles, the laundry goes wild,
Whispers of fabric, oh, what have I compiled?

A scarf chats with gloves, they gossip and sigh,
While a lonely beanie just wishes to fly.
A tangled mess of colors and flair,
Each piece has a story, quite beyond compare.

The sweater with holes claims it's fashion's new trend,
As buttons roll off, declaring their end.
Laid out on a chair, they plot and they scheme,
A lively parade of a fabric dream.

So here's to the chaos, the mismatched delight,
Where threads find a way to unwind every night.
With laughter and threads that dance to the beat,
In this silly world, we find our retreat.

Strands of Tomorrow

In a closet of blues, greens, and bright reds,
Hang clothes with ambitions of journeys ahead.
The party dress hopes for a magical night,
While pajamas just wish to stay home and write.

A belt rebels, claiming it's lost the plot,
While a loose button frets about being forgot.
Ribbons tie stories of dreams big and small,
Each fabric a whisper, a flutter, a call.

The shoelaces chatter, they twist and they turn,
Plotting adventures for which they all yearn.
A backpack's eager for trips near and far,
But stays home to nap, as it dreams of a car.

So stitch me a tale of tomorrow's fun,
Where socks dance in pairs and sunshine is spun.
In a world of fibers, each strand has its way,
Let laughter and joy lead the dance of the day.

Interlaced Journeys

A neon hoodie claims it's traveled the globe,
Witnessed wild dances while wrapped in its robe.
With zippers that giggle and pockets that hum,
Every journey traveled, a new kind of fun.

The raincoat retorts with tales from the storm,
While mittens join in, a knitted warm swarm.
Each thread has a tale, a woven reveal,
Through mishaps and laughter, it's all quite surreal.

A pair of swim trunks chat about sun,
While socks roll their eyes, "You think you're so fun?"
In the attic, old quilts share secrets from yore,
Of picnics and play, and adventures galore.

So gather your fibers, let stories unfold,
With humor and warmth, let these threads be bold.
On interlaced journeys, we laugh and we twirl,
In this fabric of life, let's give joy a whirl!

Tapestry of Hearts

In the quilt of our lives, each patch has a grin,
Even the frayed edges still shine from within.
With laughter, we stitch every moment with care,
Creating a tapestry, vibrant and rare.

The buttons hold wisdom, the zippers, a tale,
Of how mismatched soles can still learn to sail.
From fabric to fabric, our stories entwine,
With mirth in our hearts, and love as the line.

As the aprons recall all the meals that we shared,
And oven mitts chuckle of sparks that we dared.
A bit of a mess, but oh, what a sight,
In a tapestry woven with laughter and light.

So pass me the yarn, let's create something bright,
With threads of connection, our future's in sight.
In this forge of fond memories, let's play our part,
For every stitch whispers, a beat of the heart.

The Loom of Existence

In a room full of yarn, oh what a sight,
Cats chase the mayhem, pure delight.
Every color tangles, a funny dance,
Weaving mishaps lead to a chance.

Grandma's old chair creaks with glee,
Socks on the floor, just wait and see.
Knitting needles play a tune,
As stitches fly like birds in June.

A scarf turns out to be a hat,
Surprised look from the cat, imagine that!
With laughter echoing through the space,
Crafting chaos has a charming grace.

In this loom of life, we all create,
Woven smiles that won't abate.
So grab a roll, let's make a mess,
In stitches and giggles, we're truly blessed.

Silken Pathways

Threads of silk in a sunny room,
Squirmy squirrels eat patterns of doom.
Dancing spools upon the floor,
Who invited that gopher to explore?

A needle slips, and whoa, what fun!
It poked my finger; now it's a run!
Yarn balls chase each other in a race,
Laughter rings as they tumble and trace.

With every knot, stories emerge,
A tangled web of laughter and surge.
Jump in the chaos, don't be afraid,
This path of silk is humor displayed.

As colors mingle, we spin our tales,
Creating joy that never pales.
So let's embrace each floppy thread,
In this funny mess, let's forge ahead!

Threads to Tomorrow

A button here, a button there,
My shirt has more holes than a grizzly bear.
Sewing dreams with a needle's dance,
Fashion flunks, but we'll take a chance.

Threads to tomorrow, all in a whirl,
Tangled fibers make my head twirl.
Socks mismatched in a festive way,
Who knew chaos could brighten the day?

My shirt's now a vest, the hem's gone wild,
Looks like fashion got a bit riled!
With a giggle and a hug, we declare,
This fashion faux pas is nothing to wear!

But tomorrow brings hope with each funky patch,
We'll sew up the seams in a glorious match.
So here's to threads that wander and stray,
Creating humor along the way!

Cross-Stitching Moments

Cross-stitching moments, oh so bright,
Patterns unravel, what a sight!
Needles flying like a busy bee,
Stitches form chaos, just wait and see.

With each little 'x', giggles abound,
The dog thinks it's a snack all around.
Fabric frenzies stretch to the floor,
Friends join in, crafts galore!

Threads entwine in a zany loop,
As laughter echoes through our troop.
Designs get lost, colors collide,
In this crazy mess, we take pride.

So here's a toast, with needles up high,
Let's laugh at the moments that pass us by.
Cross-stitching memories, both bold and bright,
In threads of humor, we find our light!

Unraveled Truths

Mixing up colors, oh what a sight,
Socks with stripes, and dots so bright.
A sweater that's lost its hood on the way,
All tangled up in a merry ballet.

Threads of laughter, looping in time,
Each twist a story, each knot a rhyme.
Grandpa's old scarf, with tales it could tell,
If only it could, it would do so quite well.

A cat in the yarn, what a chaotic mess,
Rolling and pouncing, oh, what fun, I confess!
The more I unravel, the more laughs I weave,
In this fabric of life, I never leave.

So here's to the stitches that bound me tight,
In patterns of joy, I find pure delight.
We'll snip at the chaos, laugh at the fray,
Embracing the giggles in this bizarre display.

Bonds Beyond the Fabric

A patchwork of friends, each thread a tale,
With laughter as glue, we never can fail.
Seams may be crooked, but we hold on tight,
Creating our quilt, a colorful sight.

A friend draped in plaid, another in polka,
Unraveling secrets, like yarn from a croka.
Each stitch a promise, to stick through the flair,
In this frolicsome fabric, nothing can compare.

Silly little pranks, where fibers entwine,
A tickle with fibers, oh dear, how they shine!
We sew up the gaps with hugs and some giggles,
In this tapestry, laughter always wiggles.

So gather your threads, let the fun begin,
With colors and textures, let the laughter spin.
In this fabric of friendship, oh what a blast,
A jolly old bond, forever to last.

The Heart's Interlace

Two threads at a dance, a waltz through the night,
Twisting and turning, what a silly sight!
Fingers in knots, they're lost in a jig,
With laughter that pops, like a well-timed gig.

A quilt of confessions, the seams may break,
But together we patch, for friendship's own sake.
In stitches of humor, our hearts intertwine,
In the fabric of joy, both yours and mine.

Laughter like needles, they pierce through the gloom,
Stitching up smiles in a most vibrant room.
With patterns of merriment, life seems less tough,
In this joyful embroider, we're never enough!

So let's tidy up the mess as we chuckle more,
In this glorious weave, let's dance on the floor.
With yarns of good times and stories retold,
Let's laugh as we weave, let the magic unfold.

Layers of Life

Life's fabric layers, a mix and a match,
Some like a puzzle, some just a scratch.
Juggling the threads, oh what a parade,
A bit of a mess, but it's all homemade!

Tangled in nonsense, yet laughter runs free,
Like threads on a spool, oh just look at me!
Frayed at the edges but bright in the core,
Each stitch a giggle, who could ask for more?

Dressed in odd prints, like a patchwork of fun,
Jumping through hoops, till the day is done.
Layers of laughter, stitched tight with a grin,
Oh, this joyful chaos is where we begin!

With a spin and a twirl, as the world takes a dive,
We roll with the punches, we're clearly alive.
Each thread a reminder, to laugh through it all,
In this colorful life, together we fall.

Stitching Silence

In a quiet room, needles play,
Whispers stuck, just won't stray.
A bobbin rolls, a tiny chase,
Sewing joy with a goofy face.

Fabric shouts while threads just giggle,
Colors clash and bend, they wiggle.
A patchwork laugh, a snicker sound,
In this realm, no silence found.

Echoes of Entanglement

In a basket full of twisty fate,
Yarns in knots, they congregate.
A sweater waits, but it's bemused,
Who thought this ball was so confused?

A tangled tune of purl and knit,
Each loop a laugh, none can outwit.
With every tug, a chuckle grows,
As fabric giggles, as tension shows.

Knots of Kismet

A crafty fate, these knots unite,
Twisted tales in morning light.
Threaded puns, they tie and tease,
Silly stitches, a laugh with ease.

When sewing circles break and spin,
Laughter's bound with each new win.
A frayed edge reveals a grin,
Knots of kismet, let joy begin!

Textile Tomorrows

In fabric dreams, the future weaves,
Crazy patterns, wild beliefs.
Each stitch a hope, each fray a laugh,
Textile tales, like a silly craft.

Bobbins dance in a dizzy whirl,
Threads of jest in every twirl.
Sewing smiles with a playful heart,
In tomorrow's fabric, hilarity's art.

Fantasies in Fiber

In a closet, the yarn did conspire,
To weave dreams of a playful attire.
A hat that danced and socks that sang,
Together they laughed, as the fabric sprang.

A bright red scarf with a bold, funky twist,
Claimed it could fly—talk about gist!
The mittens high-fived with soft little sighs,
While knitting needles shot playful ties.

A sweater that whispered, 'Please wear me out!',
While buttons plotted a silly shout.
The cotton giggled, the wool rolled in glee,
A fiber party for you and for me!

So here's to the threads, with their wild antics,
Crammed full of smiles—oh, aren't they frantic?
They knit us together, through laughter and fun,
In a world of fiber where joy's never done.

Threads of Resistance

The embroidery declared a vendetta,
Against the fabric that made it better.
With stitches that tangled and knots that grew,
It waged a war, so silly too!

A spool of thread rolled under the bed,
Hoping to rise, but got tangled instead.
With a hop and a skip, it begged for a fight,
'Cause freedom felt close in the soft candlelight!

The lace croaked out protest, 'Let me be free!'
While ribbons rallied, shouting, 'Can't you see?
We're all tied down by seams that are tight!
Let's dance in loops beneath the moonlight!'

So let's cut the fabric of our hidden fears,
And stitch up our dreams with laughter and cheers.
In threads we trust, that twist and resist,
The joy of creation—impossible to miss!

The Binding of Twine

In a garden of chaos, the twine took a stand,
Claimed it could tie flowers with a flick of the hand.
But tangled up daisies began to complain,
'You're binding us all, it's such a pain!'

The roses looked on, with thorns in a huff,
Saying, 'This binding can't be too tough!
Let's weave ourselves into a glorious mess,
And have a garden party, oh, we must confess!'

With jute ropes dancing, acting rather grand,
The garden erupted, twining hand in hand.
The vines intertwined, all giggles and cheer,
'Let's bind up the laughter, we have nothing to fear!'

So gather your twine, in sweetness and fun,
In a world of connections, we're never outrun.
Let the fibers unite in a playful embrace,
And watch as we dance in this whimsical space!

Fragments and Fortitude

In a quilt of misfits, patches are stray,
Each fragment shouts, 'I matter today!'
With polka dots plotting a colorful scene,
And stripes that declare, 'We're bold and we're keen!'

The patches converged in a mad little swirl,
Chasing their friends, each thread did a twirl.
A humble old fabric piped up with pride,
'Together we're stronger—let's turn the tide!'

Swatches of laughter and snippets of cheer,
Joined in a dance, made their purpose clear.
With a stitch here and there, they fashioned a tale,
Of courage and whimsy that would never fail.

So embrace the fragments, together they thrive,
In laughter and patches, we feel so alive.
With fortitude stitched in each vibrant hue,
We weave our own stories, both funny and true!

Looping Through Memories

I tied a knot in my shoelace,
But found it in my hair,
The more I pulled, the tighter it got,
Now my head's a tangled fair!

In grandma's quilt, my dreams reside,
With cats and fish all crammed inside,
Each thread a tale of silly glee,
Stitched together, just like me.

I found a sock under the bed,
It whispered secrets, nonsense said,
We laughed so hard, it must be true,
That missing pair is laughing too!

So here's to knots and random ties,
To tangled thoughts and goofy sighs,
May every twist bring giggles near,
As memories loop like yarn, oh dear!

Threads of Hope

I spun a yarn on Friday night,
About a dog that took a flight,
With cap and goggles, soaring free,
His belly full of jellybeans, whee!

A puppet show with socks and hats,
A dance-off with my rubber bats,
Each stitch a dream, a laugh, a cheer,
Hope's in the fabric, it's all quite clear.

A ball of twine rolls down the street,
Where pigeons join and skip a beat,
With every loop, a joke in tow,
We weave together, just for show.

So gather round, let's tie this thread,
With laughter loud and visions spread,
Each silly twist, a joyful slope,
In tangled knots, we find our hope!

Binding Shadows of the Past

A shadow danced behind my chair,
It wore a hat and had no hair,
We shared a laugh, we shared a pie,
It ducked and dodged, oh me, oh my!

With tapestries of past delight,
A ghostly mime, a comical sight,
It whispered tales of yesteryear,
In half-spun jokes that disappeared.

Through every thread, a giggle grows,
Like socks that march in silly rows,
I tried to keep the laughter in,
But every stitch, my cheeks grew thin.

So here's to shadows, sly and spry,
Whose antics make the time fly by,
With threads of laughter woven tight,
Let's bind the past with sheer delight!

Weaving the Unseen

In the loom of life, we twist and spin,
With every fiber, let's begin,
To weave a joke, a playful jest,
Of silly socks, each one a guest.

A cat in yarn, a playful tease,
It thrashed about with so much ease,
We chuckled loud at its parade,
A melee of mischief — oh, the charade!

With threads of colors bright and bold,
We stitch the tales that need retold,
Each loop a laugh, a tickling sigh,
In woven whimsy, time flies by.

Let's dance through fibers, side by side,
With laughter as our joyful guide,
In every knot, a giggle spun,
As weaving tales, we all have fun!

Fables in Fabric

In a world of colors bright,
A sock tried to take flight.
With wings made of yarn and glee,
It flew right into a tree!

A hat danced low, a glove stood tall,
They laughed and played, as friends should call.
But the scarf got tangled in a kite,
Wishing it had more insight!

Then came a thread, rather bold,
With tales of adventures untold.
It spun around with joy and flair,
Woven laughter filled the air!

In this land where textiles sing,
Every loop has an amusing zing.
So stitch a smile, weave a jest,
In fabric tales, we're always blessed!

The Pull of Twists

A yarn ball rolled down the street,
Chasing a cat, oh what a treat!
It looped and danced, a silly sight,
Purring and frolicking in delight.

Two strands of thread, both blue and green,
Argued on which color is seen.
The red came in with a sassy tease,
"Both of you look like party cheese!"

A needle joined, with a wink so sly,
"I can sew chaos, oh me, oh my!"
It poked and prodded, making a fuss,
Turning the tangle into a bus!

But when the fabric met the floor,
They tumbled, giggled—what a score!
In this mess, they found their groove,
For every twist brings a chance to move!

Harmony in the Weave

A patchwork quilt of giggles galore,
Every stitch tells a story of yore.
Buttons and patches with winks and grins,
The melody of fabric always wins!

A rogue needle, sharp and sly,
Told tales of stitches that dared to fly.
"Let's break some rules, let's make a mess,
Who needs order? It's fun to guess!"

Threaded through, a bobbin danced,
Spinning in circles, it just pranced.
Laughter erupted with each little twist,
In this fabric game, none could resist!

Patterns tangled in a happy knot,
In every twist, joy can't be bought.
Together they sang, in joyous delight,
Woven harmony under moonlight!

Labyrinth of Looms

In a maze where spools all chatter,
A mix-up led to glorious clutter.
A vibrant twist and a curious turn,
In the labyrinth, there's much to learn!

A puppet thread, in search of a part,
Joined forces with fabric—now that's smart!
They wanted to dance, to sway and groove,
But round they spun, lost in the move.

A loom with ideas both quirky and bright,
Created a sweater that glowed at night.
With each tug and pull, a laugh would burst,
In the fabulous chaos, they felt immersed!

And so the fabrics had grand old fun,
As they danced in unison, one by one.
From threads of joy to tales of delight,
In this fabric maze, all felt just right!

Frayed Connections

In a world of sweaters, oh so bright,
A lone thread danced in the light.
Pull it here, and then it goes,
A non-stop game of hide and show.

My aunties chat, their yarns entwined,
While Grandpa knits, but loses his mind.
Laughter bounces, stitches slip,
A cozy mess, a fabric trip.

Colors clash in joyful dismay,
We're a patchwork quilt, come what may.
Every loop tells a story so grand,
Of tangled ties, and a goofy band.

With every pull, another thread foes,
We laugh, we cry at what life throws.
In the end, we're all quite absurd,
Frayed connections, say the word!

Interwoven Destinies

Two cats in a yarn ball, what a sight,
Tangled up, they fight and bite.
Pawns of fate, they roll and roll,
Chasing tails, losing control.

A sock on the floor, a sneeze in the air,
Mom's old chapeau without a care.
Threads go flying, the dog takes a glance,
Intertwined chaos leads to a dance.

Every twist hides a funny tale,
Of mismatched shoes and a wobbly rail.
In this fabric, laughter is sewn,
Destinies knit, yet hearts are grown.

So let's embrace the yarn's embrace,
In this silly, spinning race.
With every knot, a tale begins,
Interwoven laughter is how it spins!

Knots of Memory

Tied in knots, our memories flare,
Like shoelaces tangled, unaware.
Oh, the stories that they weave,
Of silly moments we can't conceive.

A dance-off with a vacuum's hum,
Or pies in the face, oh what fun!
Each twist reminds us of the glee,
Of crazy nights and cups of tea.

Grandma's crochet, a hit or miss,
With every knot, a laugh and kiss.
Though it may seem all in a twist,
It's the laughter we cannot resist!

So here's to knots that time forgot,
In every loop, a joyful plot.
With threads of gold, and some gray hair,
Knots of memory, beyond compare!

Unraveling Fate

Upon this spindle, fate does spin,
With every turn, where to begin?
A yarn ball rolls, and off it goes,
Chasing shadows, who knows who knows?

A jester's cap, a knotted tie,
Every twist sends laughter high.
We pull and tease, then watch it fray,
In this tangled mess, we find our play.

Through every loop, a giggle escapes,
Crazy adventures in funny shapes.
Though we tangle, and tug, and tease,
In this fabric, we do as we please.

So here's to fate, quirky and weird,
With all its knots, our hearts cheered.
In this dance of threads, we fit just right,
Unraveling fate feels so delight!

Twisted Paths of Time

In a room with socks that dance,
They twist and twirl in playful prance.
A clock ticks sideways, can't keep track,
As moments slip through, no looking back.

The cat's tied up in yarn so bright,
Chasing shadows in the moonlight.
With each new knot, a giggle blooms,
As laughter bounces off the walls and rooms.

A noodle slips from a dinner plate,
The dog's confused, it's a funny fate.
The spaghetti twists like stories told,
In a world where chaos is always bold.

So let's toast to the silly strife,
Where every snag is a slice of life.
Embrace the twists, the turns we find,
In the comedic chaos that life's designed.

Weaving Whispers

A spider spins with style and flair,
Each thread a secret, light as air.
The neighbors gossip through the night,
While tangled tales weave wrongs to right.

In a busy cafe, a straw goes wild,
Flying through hands, a paper child's.
Every sip turns into a spill,
Laughter erupts, hearts start to thrill.

Grandma's knitting goes awry,
A sweater with arms just two feet high!
She wears it proud, as smiles break free,
In a world where mishaps dance with glee.

Let's twirl in circles, take a chance,
On outfits that make the people dance.
In life's great loom, we play our part,
With tangled threads and a funny heart.

Entangled Lives

At a party, balloons take flight,
Catching ribbons in the moonlight.
One fizzles out, a squeaky sound,
Laughter explodes, joy rebounds.

In the park, a dog runs wild,
Chasing squirrels, so sweet and wild.
The leash tangles, owners fumble,
But laughter wins while mishaps tumble.

A pair of shoes, mismatched on toes,
Walking in style that nobody knows.
Trips and slips spark giggles anew,
As friends share jokes that only they do.

So let's embrace this jumbled tale,
Where adventures thrive and mishaps prevail.
In the chaos of life, we find our way,
With entangled joys that brighten the day.

Stitches of Silence

In a bazaar where silence speaks,
Stitched-up secrets hide in creeks.
A button pops, a blouse goes rogue,
The giggles spill, as tales brogue.

A mime is caught in a thread of fun,
Pretending to pull a nonexistent gun.
With jerky motions, we can't help but stare,
His own reflection gives him a scare.

Pillow fights erupt with a whoosh,
As feathers fly in a feathery push.
Every toss is a giggling prayer,
Stitches of silence fill the air.

So let us weave with silly glee,
In the quiet moments, pure jubilee.
With every stitch, a laugh we find,
In the fabric of life, with threads intertwined.

www.ingramcontent.com/pod-product-compliance
Lightning Source LLC
Chambersburg PA
CBHW060116230426
43661CB00003B/201